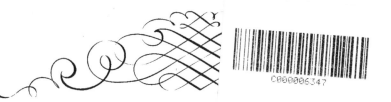

ISBN 978-1-5277-8093-4
PIBN 10894348

This book is a reproduction of an important historical work. Forgotten Books uses
state-of-the-art technology to digitally reconstruct the work, preserving the original format
whilst repairing imperfections present in the aged copy. In rare cases, an imperfection in
the original, such as a blemish or missing page, may be replicated in our edition. We do,
however, repair the vast majority of imperfections successfully; any imperfections that
remain are intentionally left to preserve the state of such historical works.

1 MONTH OF
FREE
READING

at

www.ForgottenBooks.com

By purchasing this book you are
eligible for one month membership to
ForgottenBooks.com, giving you
unlimited access to our entire
collection of over 1,000,000 titles via
our web site and mobile apps.

To claim your free month visit:

www.forgottenbooks.com/free894348

English
Français
Deutsche
Italiano
Español
Português

www.forgottenbooks.com

Mythology Photography **Fiction**
Fishing Christianity **Art** Cooking
Essays Buddhism Freemasonry
Medicine **Biology** Music **Ancient
Egypt** Evolution Carpentry Physics
Dance Geology **Mathematics** Fitness
Shakespeare **Folklore** Yoga Marketing
Confidence Immortality Biographies
Poetry **Psychology** Witchcraft
Electronics Chemistry History **Law**
Accounting **Philosophy** Anthropology
Alchemy Drama Quantum Mechanics
Atheism Sexual Health **Ancient History**
Entrepreneurship Languages Sport
Paleontology Needlework Islam
Metaphysics Investment Archaeology
Parenting Statistics Criminology
Motivational

The Elder Monthly

THOMAS L. ELDER, *Editor*

VOL. I	NEW YORK SEPTEMBER 1906	No, 7

SUBSCRIPTION PRICE FIFTY CENTS PER YEAR

Table of Contents

Editorials

Our Coins Again

If some of the Greeks who lived during the period of the best
Grecian art were again permitted to walk our streets, they would indeed
note many wonderful changes for the better.   To them the wonders of Aladdin's lamp would seem microscopic in comparison.
But what would be their emotions when, on presenting a $2 00
bill of the realm to a beanery graduate for a lunch or a "high-ball"
they received in return some of our dimes, quarters, and half dollars?   And we can imagine them looking first at the wonders of a

"Flatiron" and a Subway and then with a somewhat mystified expression at the attempts at caricature shown by the "artist" on our coins which bear the coarse, brainless female head and characterless, fantastical eagle. It is one of the most incomprehensible things that this nation now so alert to grafters and public abuses of all kinds should be entirely indifferent to such a subject as the work on the coins which we use—are compelled to use daily. The fogy idea that good enough is well enough doesn't find argument here, as our coins are far shy of "good enough." England, France, Germany, Holland, Sweden, Belgium,—yes, even little Jamaica, Hong Kong and Sarawak, have now, and have had for upwards of thirty years, better looking coins than have ever been in use in the United States. It is to be hoped that our present coins are nowise characteristic of us as a nation. How would it be for some of our well-to-do numismatists to offer a prize of say $500 or $1,000 for the best design submitted by artists for a new series of coins? This scheme ought to be feasible provided no legal technicalities were encountered. The subject is timely, must be aired constantly and should appeal to all.

George H. Earle, Jr., Numismatist

A Philadelphia numismatist now prominently before the American public as a receiver for the wrecked Real Estate Trust Company of Philadelphia, is George H. Earle, Jr. The papers are filled with news as to how this trust company was looted of well over $5,000,000 through the operations of its former President, Frank K. Hipple, who committed suicide, and who bids fair to become known as the greatest American swindler. One Adolf Segal, it is alleged, got most of the cash. Mr. Earle is one of the most enthusiastic of coin collectors. He was present at the Smith sale and bought heavily. As to Mr. Earle, the *New York Sun* says : " When the directors found there was no hope of saving the trust company and the Clearing House had refused aid, they turned to Mr. Earle. He had a reputation as a successful rehabilitator of wrecked institutions. Two or three institutions in past years had by his efforts been put on their feet again. Besides this he was the head of several large Philadelphia enterprises, among them the Finance Company. * * * Receiver Earle is a tall, lean man, with a clean shaven face that shows lines of great strength. Folks like Mr. Earle. They trust him. He is very quiet in manner and his voice is always subdued.   He is well dressed at all times but not with the modish exactness of Segal and seems to wear his clothes with a more natural grace.   Mr. Earle is still under 50, and, though he is not robust, his keen face, with its clear skin, suggests lots of outdoor exercise.''

Numismatists can, when necessary furnish the evidence that both they, and their science are very much alive.—It is a pleasure to hail Mr. Earle as ''one of us.''

The Amateur Dealer

The numismatist who proudly declines to collect or sell coins with a view of financial gain is apt to regard the small dealer in coins as a species of numismatic parasite who keeps in mind only the fattening of his purse.   Notwithstanding this the amateur merchant is really a power for good in the field of collecting, and one of its strongest props. Generally it is he who first awakens the interest of the beginner—the tyro who has never yet come in contact with the more important dealer or full-fledged collector.   The small dealer works industriously and unceasingly, because each new customer gained and collector made means to him a new source of revenue continuous for a time at least. The small dealer aids the large one by finding a place for ''junk'' lots and odds and ends which would otherwise go begging for a purchaser. It is he, who, more than anyone else, contributes to the success of a public auction sale.   His way is not always a bed of roses, either, for invariably his client sooner or later outgrows him and forsakes him for the large dealers and auction cataloguers   Thus left in the lurch, he looks around for ''new worlds to conquer,'' and generally finds them, and the dealers, the cataloguers and the science of Numismatics are benefitted.

''E. Z.'' Smith, the erstwhile mintmark shark of New Rochelle, has been laying low this summer, and but seldom does his gladsome smile brighten our door-way.   The only hint we get of his existence is through the telephone occasionally when a once melodious voice drones ''Anything new in?''   Since the ''sword of Damocles,'' or a fire-man's ax (he is a member of the N. R. volunteer fire department) dropped on his toes, he has kept quiet and this incident has also lowered his record as a base-stealer on the New Rochelle ball team.   Or did he and Mc. Graw run amuck ?

. John C. Shea, of the staff of the *Buffalo Evening News*, continues to cater to the numismatic germs through his popular "Everybody's Column," a forum for readers having an ax to grind, or an inquiry to make, or a verse to sing.   Mr. Shea prints these few don'ts for his readers:—"Don't waste paper and ink criticising other writers. Don't quarrel about race or religion.   Don't scold about matters that are beyond remedy.   Make your letters short.   More truth than fiction in such don'ts."

Benjamin Betts, the author of the well-known book on American Colonial medals is engaged in preparing a "Monograph on the medals of Admiral Vernon," which, he informs the editor, "is a work of considerable complexity, requiring a close attention to details."

The pluck of Charles E. Jenney since the bad accident which befell him leaving him minus a foot and other members, is shown by his sending us from Agnew Hospital, Kansas City, Mo., the philatelic article appearing in this issue.

C. E. Niles, President of the First National Bank, of Findlay, Ohio, has a coin collection, and is interested in curios and paper money also.   He is National Treasurer of the Independent Order of Odd Fellows.

Mr. William Poillon, curator of the A. N. & A. Society, of New York, is at work on Wednesday and Saturday afternoons of each week, at the Society's rooms, classifying the newly donated collections.

Charles Podhaiski, Charles Gregory and Edward T. Newell, well-known local collectors are enjoying European vacations at present.

Dr. Martin Burke, the well-known specialist in Greek coins, has contributed an interesting article for our October issue.

We were favored with a call recently by P. N. Breton, of Montreal, author of the well-known work on Canadian Coins.

J. Pierpont Morgan, George Gould, H. O. Havemeyer, and many other American Capitalists, have collections of coins.

F. W. Smith, a well-known stamp dealer, late of 429 Montgomery St., San Francisco, California, lost almost everything, including his stock of stamps, in the recent earthquake.

Coin and Stamp Departments have been inaugurated in the advertising columns of some of the big weekly and monthly publications, such as Colliers and Everybody's, due clearly to the growth and popularity of these branches of collecting.

The United Railroads of San Francisco, have a great relic of the recent earthquake and fire in an immense mass of melted silver, nickel and copper coins, and are at a loss to know how to go about it to get its money value back. 'Tis said this concern has suffered a greater loss through the burning of its coins than any other institution in the ill-fated city.

A Lincoln Oddity

Some time ago in my quest for Lincoln medals I was fortunate in obtaining from Mr. Davis, the curator of Roger Williams Park Museum at Providence, a very fine copy of the Lincoln "Memoria in Aeterua" or Sanitary Fair medal.

I had seen this medal before and had noticed a die crack running diagonally across the face of the martyred President but had not attached any particular significance to the defect.

This medal while being absolutely perfect bore this same die crack.

In writing to a friend who has a very complete Lincoln collection, I mentioned getting this medal and he called my attention to this die crack and asked me if I had noticed that it took the exact course of the assassin's bullet, entering the head at the eye, running diagonally across and leaving the head at the base of the brain. This is the exact location of the crack and it seems almost prophetic, foreshadowing as were the fate of one of the grandest men this or any other country ever produced.—ROBERT P. KING.

The Use of Silver in the Kingdom of Annam

Written for the MONTHLY by Howland Wood, Secretary of the American Numismatic Association.

As in so many of the far Eastern countries silver has paid but a small part in the monetary system of Annam. Indeed the energies of the successive Annamese rulers, when they have seriously bothered their heads concerning the currency, have been directed almost wholly in supplying the people with a rather inferior cash or sapeque. We know that until very recently China has been content to mint for its people only bronze or copper cash, the silver in use consisting of foreign dollars, broken silver and ingots made with a semi-official sanction by rich families, banking establishments and Mandarins. As Annam has for centuries been more or less under Chinese control we are, naturally, not greatly surprised to find the conditions in the southern monarchy similar to those in the great middle kingdom. A glance through the numismatic history of Annam will reveal a great variety of bronze or zinc cash, smaller and thinner than the Chinese cash. We find that for centuries the Chinese mints made an inferior cash, similar in inscription to their own, for use in Annam. However, for transactions calling for large amounts these strings of cash would be very bulky and inconvenient, silver, and even gold would have its use. Undoubtedly in very early times, gold dust, lumps nuggets and ingots of the precious metals passed by weight. The cast ingots gradually took certain forms and bore certain marks. Just when the change took place we don't know.

The first officially inscribed bars or ingots met with were made during the reign of Gia Long, who ruled for twenty years beginning with 1801. His two successors continued these issues. The next ruler, Tn Duc, issued these bars very sparingly and then only in the smaller sizes. At times some of these latter pieces with the names of one of the four rulers minting them come up in auction sales. They cannot, however, be classed as real money, they being rather Treasury pieces kept in this form as a reserve. Their circulation was very limited in Annam as they were nearly always hoarded away by rich families. Undoubtedly they were more frequently seen outside of the country than in it.

These official ingots came in many sizes and weights, the commoner varieties are: Nen bac, weighing 10 Taels; Nua nen bac, weighing 5 Taels; Luong or dinh bac, a tenth of a Nen and weighing

1 Tael; a Nua luong or half Tael, and a quarter luong weighing 9.762 grammes. These bars are rectangular and have on one side the title of the reign and sometimes the year in which they were issued. surrounded by a decorative border; on the other side the value of the piece, and often the name of the place where made. The lengths and thicknesses of these pieces vary with the different reigns and oftentimes within the same reign. One cannot draw any conclusions by the values imprinted on them. as the values and weights oftentimes do not correspond. Somewhere on the piece is generally stamped the marks of the comptroller of the treasury. Some of the pieces seem to have been cast while others appear to have been struck. There are also some pieces of this order in gold, one of the largest known is in the mint collection at Paris, and weighs nearly eight and a half pounds.

There is however a bar of silver that circulates more or less freely, not only in Annam but Cambodia, Burmah and the Shan States. This is generally known as the commercial Nen and is of private manufacture, similar to the "shoes" used in China. It is about four and a half inches long, a little over an inch broad, and about three-quarters of an inch thick. As a rule, it is slightly curved and is concave on one of its sides; Often the weight and makers name are punched or engraved in the piece. It generally passes current at about $15.50. These pieces vary slightly in different localities. The farther west they are made the shape changes more radically, until we get the Shan baw and the as'ek types of the Sao States and the spherical ticals of Siam.

We now come to a class of silver coins that may be called actual money, but unfortunately for numismatic interests the issues were limited and but of short duration. Under the reign of Minh Mang, which was between the years of 1821 and 1840, an issue of round flat silver coins was attempted. They were patterned after the European dollars or piastres that were so current everywhere in the East. They were first issued in 1832 and were called in Annam Tam bac-tron or "round silver," and Bac-chien phi, or "dragon silver" coins. These pieces failed of a great success as the metal in them was so base, and in consequence proved very hard to find a ready acceptance. The best of the dollars did not contain over 62.5 parts of pure silver, and not a few of them had much over 37.5 parts of silver. Although these piastres are seldom found in Annam they are not especially rare in other countries. The issue was of two sizes, piastres and half piastres, and have on the obverse, in the centre, a radiant sun surrounded by four characters indicating the reign. The reverse has the imperial five toed dragon surrounded with frames. The next two rulers continued to strike the half piastres, but only to a limited extent. Many people consider these smaller pieces as medals. A very limited number were struck in gold, weighing half a Tael. Since the French intervention all of this money has gradually been done away with, its place being taken by large issues of the "piastre de commerce" and its sub-divisions, minted at Paris for French Indo China.

Before leaving the subject of silver money some mention should be made of a large series of medals that have been issued in Annam for a long time. They come in gold, silver and bronze and are generally round and with a central hole. These pieces are often considered as coins, but there is no ground for this assumption. Occasionally they may have had a limited circulation, but even then only by weight the same as any lump or ingot of metal would have. The obverse of these medals bear as a rule the same characters as found on the current cash of Minh-Mang and Thieu-Tri, hence the error in considering them coins. The reverses have a variety of inscriptions and designs. Some of the subjects depicted on these medals are, the heavens with the sun and moon surrounded by clouds; the firmament and the earth covered with trees and flowers and the sea and the mountains, together with the inscription "The four beautiful things." Others have fishes on either side of the central hole while still others have shells, bats, sceptres, swasticas and other symbols. Their inscriptions alone would preclude their attribution as money. A few are given herewith: "The three aged [ministers of the state of Lu]." "To render the people rich and long lived," "May my people be happy," "Honor is the first virtue," "Five felicities," etc.

The question naturally arises: For what use are these medals, they do not express concrete thoughts nor do they depict or commemorate current or historical events; rather do they illustrate abstract ethical maxims. As eastern courts do not cater to popular sentiment they feel no need of commemorating passing events, as great victories, royal marriages and births, hence they intrench themselves behind the bulwarks of their theocratic monarchal existence and deal out to the people aged maxims culled from the great writings of the past. The medals are distributed more as the decorations and orders are bestowed on people by the Occidental nations. Bravery in the wars, virtuous living, services rendered the state, the giving of money to the treasury by rich men, and many other good and ample reasons cause these medals to be distributed. New Years day and other national festivals are the chief occasions when these medal are dissipated.

However, nearly all cabinets of any pretentions in the line of far eastern numismatics display a few examples of these different emissions from Annam, and no one who has ever seen a collection of this kind will deny that the otherwise monotonous sequence of the regular cash is made far more interesting by the interpolation of these odd and curious bits of silver.

—

Magnificent Jewelry of Ancient Greece, Now in New York

Jewels that were worn twenty four hundred years ago are indeed worth more than passing study! And some of these have just come to New York. They have been purchased for the Metropolitan Museum of Art from the Rogers Fund and are now to be seen in the magnificent gold room of the museum. They are among the choicest in that collection of gems, for the workmanship is as fine as any by modern hands, and no one knows how many thousand dollars would be needed to buy these splendid specimens from the Museum. In fact, they are beyond price, for they could not be duplicated, and any society belle would be safe in wearing these, as no one could or would match them.

Other Greek jewels have been found here and there, but none in any museum in the world, not even in Greece, are any finer, if as fine, as these now in New York. All were found in one grave, but for certain reasons it is not stated when or where they were found. The laws of Greece are very strict about the exportation of antiques, and it would not do to say when or where these were found, as the Greek government might apply for the return of the jewels. And they are too valuable to surrender. This collection was buried with some dame of high rank of ancient Athens, probably at her special request, because her jewels were most precious and she did not like to think of any other woman wearing them after she was dead and buried.

The jewels are well preserved and show that the ancient Greeks cared little for precious stones, but preferred instead artistic forms of pure gold. These jewels include a diadem, a necklace, a pair of earrings, a finger ring, seven rosettes in the form of a flower and nineteen beads from a necklace. They are all of the yellow gold which the Greeks used for their finest jewels It is certain from their style and workmanship that these splendid specimens of the goldsmith's art date from the fifth century B. C., when Greece was at her best artistically, when Pericles was ruler and Phidias and his school set up miracles of art that the world has never since equalled, much less surpassed.

The diadem is a very thin plate of gold 14½ inches long and 2⅛ inches wide in the centre. Its decorations are entirely of repousse work hammered into carefully modelled low reliefs. In the centre the youthful Dionysos and Ariadne are sitting back to back, their faces turned toward each other. Each holds a staff with a pine cone at the top, the thyrsos, which was the sacred emblem of Dionysos and his followers. They are seated on a conventionalized design of akanthos leaves, from the centre of which a large flower rises. Large scrolls run to the ends of the diadem, terminating in the honeysuckle pattern, and between the scrolls are small female figures seated on the stalk of the vine from which the scroll springs.

These small figures, five on each side, are beautifully modelled, no two being alike, even the features differing. It is possible that these are meant to represent the Muses, those on the two sides being considered duplicates. On each side the first is playing upon the small Greek harp, the second holds a pair of pipes, the third plays a lyre, the fourth sings from a scroll and the fifth is playing a lute. There are flowers among the scrolls, three birds on the ground and even grass hoppers are to be distinguished on the flowers.

The necklace consists of a closely woven braid of fine gold wire, from which the pendants hang by intertwined chains, with rosettes at the point of attachment. There are three rows of pendants in the shape of amphora, pointed at the bottom. Those in the upper row are quite small, linked directly to the ornaments below the braid; those of the middle row are somewhat larger, and hang on small chains, with a tiny disc where chain and pendant join; those of the lowest row are much larger and most elaborate in design and finish. In this row each pendant is hung by two chains, and the chains are fastened by rosettes to both the pendant and the braid above.

The rosettes are marvels of workmanship, each being double, consisting of a large five petalled flower with another smaller flower wrought on top of it. Although the flowers are so small and close together, there is a very fine gold wire around the edge of each petal delicately soldered to it. It is probable that these leaves were originally beautifully enameled, but this has long since worn off. Still finer than the flowers and so small that a strong glass is needed to study them are the foreparts of winged griffins. These are excellent examples of the Greek devotion to art for art's sake, for the griffins add so little to the general effect that they seem hardly worth all the trouble. These little animals are modelled by hand, not stamped or cast. The two clasps are exceedingly artistic, and the whole is remarkably well preserved. The necklace is only twelve and five-eighths inches long, so it could not have been worn loosely, but must have been worn like a collar, close to the neck.

The earrings are as remarkable as the necklace for design and execution. They are three inches long, and consist of three parts. At the top is a disc decorated with an elaborate filigree rosette; from this hangs a crescent, and from the crescent hang three rows of pendants like those of the necklace, with the double rosettes and winged griffins where they are attached, are notable for extreme and unusual detail. the pistils and stamens being represented exactly after nature. As a whole, this collection of jewels is equalled in few museums and surpassed by none, even in Greece itself. If a society belle of our day could only purchase a necklace and earrings like these she would proudly show them as of greater artistic value than any gorgeous diamonds worn by others of her set, and her jewels would be quite as costly, for these command high prices on account of their antiquity as well as their intrinsic value.

Who wore these jewels? What was the name of the beautiful woman who ordered them buried with her body, that she might wear them for centuries? No one will ever be able to tell this secret, but it is not difficult to reconstruct the personality that must have claimed such jewels in the period when Greece led all the civilized world in producing the most artistic statues, buildings, even jewels, that have never since been equaled.—*N. Y. Herald.*

A Marcy (N. Y.) collector writes, "I have a very fine 10c piece, and four coins coined 210 years B. C., coined when Venus ruled." Willie Armstrong, of Ohio, asks for bottom quotations on "Gold double-eagle of 1849; half eagles of 1815 and 1822; silver dollar of 1804; and dime of 1804, with 'S' under wreath." Hobbs, Md. addresses the editor as "Dear Unknown Friend," and did not forget to remind him that his 1808 half dollar belonged to his great-grandmother. He adds "the gold dollar is so precious that I could not mark the date very plainly, but it is 1852 nevertheless."

Send us 50 cents for a year's subscription to THE ELDER MONTHLY. It will be a paying investment. Read what is doing in Numismatics, Philately and Archæology. Bright, pointed, timely articles of interest to all. We aim to avoid lengthy and lifeless articles on extinct and inane subjects. You can't keep in touch with what the Societies are doing without THE ELDER MONTHLY.

Stamp Notes

Written for the MONTHLY by Charles E. Jenney.

The next few years will, without doubt, witness a great deal of interest by collectors in the current issue of stamped envelopes. The great variation in many of these from the original die, caused by the re-touching or re-engraving, has been noticed by everyone and only the fact of its being so common a stamp has prevented it from being much talked and written about. This is a frequent mistake of collectors; if a stamp is scarce or rare and a minute variety of it is discovered, great interest centres around it and everybody waits to secure it; but in a common stamp we see by scores every day, any variations are often overlooked and not considered worth bothering over.

That this is a mistake is evidenced by the history of the envelope stamps of 1857, 1861 and 1864. Although collectors had always recognized that there were many differences in the size and position of the letters on these stamps, they did not take the trouble to study them carefully or to preserve any of the varieties until just a few years ago one of our specialists took these issues up carefully and published an article describing their varieties. Only then was our attention withdrawn from the search for foreign minor varieties and we began to try to complete our collection of the more marked varieties of these envelopes, but alas! in the meantime all our stock of duplicates of these stamps had gone and many of the varieties that had doubtless been owned by us in the past, could no longer be found, and the prices in the catalogue were increased.

Let us learn wisdom from the past and not let history repeat itself in this current stamp. Every collector has probably saved up a few marked varieties and has only awaited for a comprehensive classification to be made of them by some authority. Such has been attempted by Mr. Louis G. Barrett and was published in *Mekeel's Weekly Stamp News*, although, as he says, it is too early, before an issue is retired to compile a complete list, as not only is it probable that more retouches will be made, but even more frequently on account of the age and longer use of the dies.

Mr. Barrett already makes seventy different types of retouched dies so it will be seen there is an ample field for investigation. This seems an enormous number and not at all warranted even with the great wear they must be subject to in printing all our 2 cent envelopes for a space of three years. It would seem, that with so many varieties that no man can tell them all, it would be easy for the counterfeiter to manufacture them undetected and doubtless this consideration will, as well as their lack of artistic merit, soon bring about a new issue of stamped envelopes. Then we will all be sorry if we have not saved as many as possible of the die varieties.

* * *

Probably few stamp issues ever suffered so severely from any one disaster as did the California State Revenue stamps in the San Francisco earthquake and fire. California collectors were naturally interested in the already scarce issues of their own state and consequently many large collections and stocks were held in San Francisco. One of the largest of these, that of W. F. Greany, was found consumed by heat when his safe was opened. Many other lots were destroyed. Of course there are some fine collections of these state revenues owed outside of California but they are few. Moreover the undiscovered stock, that on original documents and the only source on which collectors had to draw, was almost entirely in San Francisco.

* * *

More collectors than one would suppose are collecting the printed permits under which 2nd and 3rd class mail matter is now mailed. They seem fully as collectable as the so-called "Penalty envelope" franks of the different departments though these, strangely enough, were sadly overlooked by collectors. One drawback to the collecting of these permits is that they must be kept entire and the great variation in their size makes them inconvenient for arranging or displaying.

* * *

With a history like hers, it seems a little strange to us that Greece should go to the Olympic games for designs for her postage stamps. Several such issues have already appeared and they are still coming. Should she not rather go to Olympus itself or honor the Homeric heroes.

* * *

Panama is attracting as much attention in the philatelic world as the canal-digging is to the world at large. A few years ago only a province of the U. S. of Columbia, to-day it is an independent country whose stamp issues number in the hundreds.

Greek Coin Types

[CONTINUED FROM LAST ISSUE.]

But it would be dangerous to press this view far, or we should have to adopt the absurd hypothesis that the value unit of Theos had once been the griffin, or that of Milletus the lion, since these are the first representations found on their coinages, both of which go back to the very first days of the invention of money.

Mr. Macdonald rejects both these accepted views in favor of the simple theory that the early coin type merely reproduces the state seal of the issuing state. The community vouched for the purity and good weight of the piece by sealing it with the device which it habitually appended to documents, etc. As was the case in the cities of mediæval Europe, many states used religious emblems as their coat of arms, but others used commercial types and others again "canting heraldry," making a pun on the city name, without any religious or other *arriere pensee*. Thus, to compare things ancient with things modern, Athens used Athene's owl, or Ephesus the stag of Artemis, just in the same way as the city of London uses the red cross with St. Paul's sword in the canton, or Venice uses the lion of St. Mark. On the other hand Cyzicus used the tunny or Cyrene the silphium plant as purely commercial devices, illustrating the chief industry of the city as much as Bristol shows the castle and ship, Canada the Beaver or Iceland the stock-fish in its shield. But quite distinct from each of these we get the punning type. Trapezus showed a table on its coins, Ancona an elbow, Selinus a parsley leaf, just as Oxford now gives us an ox fording a river, Bern a bear or Munich a monk. It seems to us that this lucid, simple, yet many-sided explanation of the early coin types is absolutely conclusive. It leaves us with many religious emblems, such as the one school of commentators pointed out, and many commercial emblems to please the other, yet shows that the type of the coin is only religious or commercial at second hand, so to speak. It reproduced the state seal, and the device of that seal might be settled by either of the two tendencies which prevailed among the early choosers of a municipal device, or might even be settled by mere canting heraldry.

—Saturday Review.

When writing advertisers please mention THE ELDER MONTHLY.

...v and ⅛ ...ning, ...each ...bright red, and 2c; Holland, ½c; 15

fine, scarce ...upee, uncirculated, each. Choice,each. 50

...ollar, "1299," fine, rare ......, each 35c, lot. 05

...ree slate double thaler.................... 50

...gland dollar, heavy, fine 80

...la dollar, George III, fine 85

Victoria dollar 1 50

...anuel de Rohan, about fine, scarce 1 25

...own with armoured bust, good 30 tari or dollar, scarce 1 75

uncirculated................................... 75

e cents, 1857 and '58, 30 for. 1 80

...federate and State bills, poor to unc, per 100 1 40

1 $10 bills, (good) per 100 1 50

...rrency, good condition, 10c, bills, 18c, 25c, 30c, 50c, 1 50

t made when a quantity is bought. 1 00

...native nickel issue   Scarce, each 1 50

...sh coins, now obsolete, each 1 75

er, fine, each. 12

...rovincial coppers, also new imperial issue, (not cash 10

.... 10

...s, about 6 varieties mixed, all bright red, unc.50 for 1 60

, unc. in lots of 6, each 65

...liars, always in demand, 1806, '07, very fair, each 70

1835, shows a fine date, and scarce, each 2 00

...ld Dollars. Uncirculated. each 1 90

...me. Good. Very rare 1 50

...s, in lots of 3, each 80

...5c nickel, date 1877. Proof. each 3 50

3. Proof. Very rare 3 50

...77. Unc. Rarer than proof. Each 1 00

...s, guaranteed over 1600 years old, good condition,

for 1 00

...up coins. Very thick and irregular. Good speci-

ties for 1 00

...als at $2 to $25 apiece. Will send on approval to respon-

...Emeralds suitable for mounting, $5 to $20 each. Tur-

..., at $1 to $3 apiece, according to size. Cut India garnets

...s at $1 and $2 each. Opal and sapphire rings for sale.

...r and fair, $2.75 per 100. U.S.white cents (1859-64)good

Lewis and Clark Gold ¼ dollar souvenir, 50 cents. U.

...very scarce, fine, each $1.25.

...c Private or Foreign gold, silver and copper coins,

...illustrating and pricing thousands of

...retail selling list free.

CPSIA information can be obtained
at www.ICGtesting.com
Printed in the USA
BVHW061655031218
534640BV00037B/3831/P